To Poetry, With Love

Sangeeta Chakladar

BookLeaf Publishing

India | USA | UK

Presentation by *BookLeaf Publishing*

Web: www.bookleafpub.com

E-mail: info@bookleafpub.com

ISBN:9789360940997

First edition 2024

DEDICATION

I dedicate this book of poems to the loving memory of my Ma and Baba. They strongly inculcated in me the passion for reading and taught me to see the world through my own kaleidoscope.

ACKNOWLEDGEMENT

An endeavor of any kind always needs a strong support system. For my book "To Poetry, With Love" to see the light of day I have received constant love and encouragement from my family. My son, Rishabh has been my biggest support in my passion for writing. He doubles up as my editor, technical support and also constantly nudges me to write more. My daughter, Ruchita has been the best cheerleader, always with a kind word of appreciation. Robin, my husband, is my strong critic and all-time companion. Without my strong family, this book would not have been possible. A heartfelt Thank you to my family. A humbling gratitude to BookLeaf Publishing for creating this opportunity to make this book happen.

PREFACE

My book of poems is like a window to my various emotions and observations. Emotions, like a roller coaster, have been tranquil to turbulent and they largely reflect in my work through the pages of this collection of poems. I wrote these poems driven by my musings in different phases of time. The roles I have played in my life of being a woman, a literature student, a daughter, an Army Officer's wife, a mother and a traveller have largely influenced my individuality and in turn, have seeped into my style of writing. I am essentially a storyteller by nature and this doesn't escape my poetry either. I wish and hope my poems touch some cord of resonance in my reader's heart and mind.

Table of Contents

Fading

I am fading, like the silk threads of a fraying old shawl,
I am fading, like the peeling paint on your backyard wall,
I am fading, like the fragile pages of an unopened book,
I am fading, like the folded maps of roads I never took.

I am fading, like the sounds of those long unheard voices,
I am fading, like the failures of my ruthless youthful choices,
I am fading, like the lone calendar hanging way past its date,
I am fading, like the wilting yellow grass under a tree's shade.

I am fading, like my own shadow losing its way in the dark,
I am fading, like the painting, unframed and watermarked,

I am fading, like the crumbling sepia photos in
an old album,
I am fading, like a childhood memory lost in
life's humdrum.

I am fading, like the hidden heart-beat of a first
secret love,
I am fading, like the letters forgotten in the black
trunk above,
I am fading, like the autumn leaf withering in
winter's slumber,
I am fading, like my reflection in a tarnished
mirror, with nothing left to forget or remember.

An Ode To The Martyrs

The world did not shatter, life in the alleys still
went on,
But a few brave soldiers fighting bravely had
forever gone.
They roared like real heroes before they were
finally slain,
The cowardly militants kept hiding, not ready to
refrain.
Terror envelopes a beautiful valley, which we all
call heaven,
Soaked in ruthless bloodshed, this land is now
laden.

There were talks and debates and newsroom hours,
There were candles, marches and coffins with
flowers.
The tricolor was being honored, but there was a
price to pay,
The wounds of pain, the emptiness of death, were
here to stay.
The grief of this nation, the grief of the loss of
your own,
Are we shamed and guilt-ridden or have we turned
to stone.
How many more martyrs will have to finally die,
For our national flag to sway against the blue sky.

My Soldier

You look like a crawling line of ants marching
along the rugged hills.
You know there is enemy waiting ahead, yet you
don't forget your drill.
Soldier, I know you.

You surge along even when the feet are aching
and shoulder stoops.
You are the brave Indian soldier, you are the
marching troops.
Soldier, I know you.

You guard the mighty Himalayas and the barren
desert sand.
You do not care for the terrain, for in it you see
your motherland.
Soldier, I know you.

You are the brave heart who surmounts obstacles
through thick and thin.
You come back home sometimes on foot,
sometimes in the coffin.
Soldier, I know you.

You are not only a name on my day's paper, or a
face on the screen.
You care not for all this glamour, for you were
never meant to be seen.
Soldier, I know you.

You are my friend's dear husband someday, or a
neighbour's darling son.
No battle was lost without you, no war without
you could ever be won.
Soldier, I know you.

You don your uniform with valour with or
without the medal.
You are also the tender father to the baby in the
cradle.
Soldier, I know you.

You are standing like a strong wall along the line
of control.
You are the reason I sleep in peace, you are my
strong console.
Soldier, I know you.

You do not die in the call of duty, you save the
life of others.
You are the pride of my nation, of the mothers
and the fathers.
Soldier, I salute you.

Resilience

A story of a nation,
Leaning on the mighty Himalayas and
Hindukush,
Which fought to stop every invaders' push.

A story of a nation,
Seeing the world walk into its inner courtyard,
Believing in the silk routes' trading facade.

A story of a nation,
With resilience and valor trying to save its lands,
Saving its integrity from the tight grip of the
British hands.

A story of a nation,
To stand up with head held high, after each
battle pain,
To uphold deep-seated resilience, time and
again.

A story of a nation,
Which marched for Swaraj with a steel resolve
of tolerance,
Broken in two and yet celebrated independence.

A story of a nation,
Often dwindling and crumbling into fragmented
quarters,
And building again from those gathered mass of
shatters.

A story of a nation,
Where amidst unity thrives diversity's endless
scope,
Where hearts are filled with strong resilience
and hope.

A story of a nation,
Where a resilient populace marks its presence
strong,
Swaying the national flag and singing the
national song.
This is the story of my country, young but
centuries old.
My nation is my pride, and has endless stories
untold.

Void Within

When there is a void within,
No happy thoughts can knock.
When there is a void within,
Every smile seems to mock.
When there is a void within,
Roads neither meet nor cross.
When there is a void within,
All thoughts drown in pathos.
When there is a void within,
No garden bloom looks blushed.
When there is a void within,
Voices around are softly hushed.
When there is a void within,
Music brings melancholic tears.
When there is a void within,
Eyes brim with untold fears.
When there is a void within,
Sunshine does not touch.
When there is a void within,
Vision blurs in raindrops' smudge.

Wake up and fill your void
With purpose and delight
Wake up and fill your void
With the maker's glorious light.

When there is a void within,
Seek another lonely soul.
When there is a void within,
To bring a smile, be your goal.
When there is a void within,
Fill it up with faith and trust.
When there is a void within,
Stand stoic against wind's gust.
When there is a void within,
Flow like the river flows.
When there is a void within,
Grow like a tiny grass grows.
When there is a void within,
Sit with a child at play,
When there is a void within,
Splash the canvas with colors spray.
When there is a void within,
Travel like a grain of sand from desert to sea,
When there is a void within,
Let your self soar high and set its chains free.

I Am The Buyer

For long they have been selling their dreams
And I am the buyer.
For long their slogans churn the stream
And I am the buyer.
They sold harvest, they sold gold.
They sold Marx, brave and bold.
They sold a comrade, they sold voice.
They sold placards, deafening noise.

They sold the darkness of a damp cell,
What was I buying I could no more tell.

For long they have been selling their thoughts
And I am the buyer.
For long their slogans brewing wrought
And I am the buyer.
They sold wisdom, they sold help
They sold freedom, but not for self.
They sold praise, they sold fire,
They sold a future with a date to expire.

They sold a world down in a well,
What was I buying I could no more tell.

For long they have been selling their faith,
And I am the buyer.
For long their slogans igniting wrath
And I am the buyer.
They sold agitation, they sold purification
They sold terror, they sold fear.
They sold the hearts of someone dear.
They sold religion to suit their region.

They sold faith in a closed shell,
What was I buying I could no more tell.

For long they have been selling their progress
And I am the buyer.
For long their slogans deepening in regress
And I am the buyer.
They sold commotion, calling it revolution.
They sold racism, burying humanism.
They sold a house with a rigid wall.
They sold a market where values fall.

They sold a heaven which looked like hell,
What was I buying I could no more tell.

For long they have been selling potions of power
And I am the buyer.
For long their slogans of decaying desire
And I am the buyer.
They sold knowledge of a twinkling land
They sold a world within your hand.
They sold restless, jaded generation
They sold youth without passion.

They sold a soul which can not sell,
What was I buying I could no more tell.

Riot

The doors and windows were closed tight,
Children looked lost, their fathers paled in fright,
Mothers sat stone cold, waiting the impending
doom,
Bereft of sunshine the room was sinking in
gloom.

They sat huddled, shaking, not daring a
whimper,
The silence was deep, no words to whisper,
Their tiny rooms were no fortress-walled,
The mayhem outside could no more be stalled.

The rioters were no strangers, they were brothers
and kin,
They killed in the name of religion, their rage
was not a sin,
Bathed with the blood of friends, with no sense
of treason,
Their thoughts, anger, violence, was brewing
like slow poison.

With red hands and bloodshot eyes, they felt like
a messiah,
With no guilt or shame or pain they turned into a
pariah,
Anger was their only religion, revenge was what
they sought,
Mere puppets in the hands of power, easily sold
and bought.

The raging fire by night would subside by the
new dawn,
Mangled, mauled, heaped bodies but none left to
mourn,
Empty roads soaked in red, sole witness of the
gory night,
A tale too brutal to be put in words, yet staring
in naked sight.

When will humanity learn the futility of killing
and rape?
A child born on that night of pain, how will his
life shape?
Will he grow with the stories of peace or of
human hate?
In that little mind can we sow the good and
await a better state?

Chorus

The "Me too" waves were reaching the shore,
Hush, they said, make noise no more.
The child is sleeping, don't wake her up,
For she doesn't know that she can join the hub.

Two frail hands raised, as she cried "Me too",
I looked around and saw a face of sixty-two.
Oh quiet lady, your story has passed expiry date,
She would not know, her beginning itself was
late.

That girl sleeping on the streets, every night,
She did not know "Me too" was a fight.
The village homes, the urban flats,
Who is counting the "Me too" stats.

They sat huddled, under the red light,
Their glittering dresses, telling of their plight.
Their chorus whisper was turning pretty loud,
Were they entitled to join the "Me too" crowd?

We are sorry, we took time to speak,
We are sorry, our strength was bleak.
In collective voice we gather strength,
We forgot to measure time's wavelength.

We will not justify reasons for the delay,
For it is not a game of sprint or relay.
Look into our eyes and own up guilt,
Let us see your manhood wilt.

Me too is not a voice or a body shamed,
Me too is in our mind of a face unnamed.
Me too is a call, to twist the hand that caused us
pain.
Me too is a mission to obliterate our mental
stain.
Me too is not a fashionable trendsetter,
Me too is not to make the women feel better.
Me too is not the salt running down with tears,
Me too is the salt of grit and march, to overcome
hidden fears.
Me too is a story to be voiced and told,
By the most powerful amongst us and the
beautifully bold.

Hope of dusk

The nights were sombre, days were grim,
Dawn was clothed like sleep's old pimp.
The thoughts were crowded, smiles were hidden,
Laughter was scarce, perhaps forbidden.

I walked a mile to meet the dusk.

The children had forgotten to run and play,
Parents had locked them in homes to stay.
The neighbors were fearful, doors were shut,
The houses looked barren like some abandoned
hut.

I walked a mile to meet the dusk.

The friends had left, families had forgotten,
Humanity was alone waiting to be rewritten.
The sick were in pain, breathing was not easy,
Yet the air flowed freely, light and breezy.

I walked a mile to meet the dusk.

Dusk was filled with birds chirping sound,
A joyous melody of hearts homeward bound.
Dusk cradled in its arms the sun and moon,
Dusk showered the earth with a celestial boon.

I walked a mile to meet the dusk.

Dusk was waiting for me at the bend of lane,
Holding in one hand, a sunset framed.
Dusk showed me in that beautiful light,
A hope for tomorrow, burning ever so bright.

I had walked a mile to meet the dusk.

Melting

The mountain peaks at dawn, glistening like a
white dress,
From my perched window, it seemed to be
heaven's address;
Melting in the warmth of day, the glacier
softening its snow,
Meandering along gently forward, yet none
could see it flow.

I gazed and gazed and in my heart,
I felt some desires melting away, like the
flowing snow!

The sun softly coloured the western sky in
molten gold,
I stood transfixed seeing the hues, which the
rays had unfold,
Each ray of warm crimson, slowly melting into
the deep lake,
Touching the core of every ripple, till it bled red
with ache.

I gazed and gazed and in my heart,
I felt some deep-seated anger melting away, like
a pain waiting to go!
Evening Azaan from a far away mosque filled
the air around,
The praise of Allah permeating and melting;
music profound!
I turned away from the window, and walked into
my room,
To light a candle at my altar, to fill it with
jasmine bloom.

I gazed and gazed and in my heart,
I felt some greed melting away, with the ebbing
echoes by the evening light!

The melting candle at the altar, drops of wax
gently pouring,
In meditative silence I waited, to feel the
heartbeats soaring,
Soaring into those lofty realms where the mind
begs to reside,
In the lap of nature, in a world without any
forceful divide.

I gazed and gazed and in my heart,
I felt some attachments melting away, in that
darkness of the night!

The darkness of the night indulging the
sparkling stars,
From dawn to night I stood and stared into a
horizon very far.
I melted with the hours and followed the day
like a sage,
I learned from every spec bestowed upon earth's
endless stage.

I gazed and gazed and in my heart,
I felt some pride melting away, in that humbling
silence of gratitude.

Desert Muse

A grain of sand has been calling out to me,
Has been calling out to me since eternity.

Since eternity I am waiting to meet,
Waiting to meet through rain and sleet.

Through rain and sleet, through heat and dust,
Through heat and dust my wait and trust.

My wait and trust for my love for a land,
My love for a land, where there is a grain of
sand.

A grain of sand, with endless miles to run,
Endless miles to run in the blazing sun.

In the blazing sun with the glistening light,
With the glistening light on a full moon night.

On a full moon night without any sleep,
Without any sleep in my dreams it will seep.

In my dreams it will seep a grain of sand,
A grain of sand from the desert land.

From the desert land to the shores of the sea,
To the shores of the sea I roam in search of thee.

In search of thee, yet you slip through my hand,
You slip through my hand, a twinkling grain of
sand.

A twinkling grain of sand, holding time in an
hourglass,
In an hourglass, eternity shall come and gently
pass.

Shall come and gently pass the echoing calls to
me,
The echoing calls to me, is a mirage of my
destiny.

A mirage of my destiny, the desert calls and I
cannot refuse,
I cannot refuse, for it is buried deep within me,
my desert muse.

The Ghats

Ruins from centuries and the glory of Bhole Nath,
A river named Ganga which has travelled its path.
Bangles of glass in rainbow colours making a
chime,
As the weavers' weave makes silk threads sublime.
Mute spectator-like ghats have untold stories to
tell,
Where myth and history mingle and sentiments
dwell.
The Ghats stand stoic as Ganga splashes away,
Perhaps in angry protest against the deepening
clay.
Steps descent, one by one to reach the river bed,
With each step ego, self, quests are gently shed.
Threadbare one stands in neck-deep waters,
To swim or simply float, it no more matters.
Every step is drenched with the footprints of my
kin,
Slippery with the sediments of some ancient sin.
As evening sets, crowds gather around the
euphoric shore,
Boats sway in mid river till the river can hold no
more.
Worship begins as hundred lamps light up the
river,
Chants of Vedic shlokas adding fervour and shiver.

Not far from there another light burns beautifully bright,
Flames from the funeral pyre dancing in shameless delight.
The mourners' muffled cries are not to be heard here,
For death by this ghat was perhaps the last desire.
Death parades hand in hand with life, day and night,
The forever burning fire is a reminder of that truth, in open sight.
To attain moksha and freedom from the cycle of life,
The path is arduous and not many are ready for the strive.
The labyrinth of narrow winding lanes leading up to open spaces,
Symbolic of the heart, mind, faith and trust of human races.
The charm of the ghats, the temples, the river flowing deep,
All drenches the soul and forever in our memories Varanasi seeps.

A Beach

The waves had long receded, the beach was
breathing free,
The tiny crabs drawing on the wet sand, a
beautiful tapestry.

But the high tides soon brings the thrashing
waves back,
Rushing in and washing away every trace in its
track.

Shells hiding a life within, waiting for the waves
to return,
Journey's back into the depths, where the deep
waters churn.

Left back on the beach are some broken,
abandoned shells,
Whispering tiny echoing sighs as the raging
water swells.

Footprints on the sand are but guests, who will
not stay,
Whatever written on the shores soon gets
washed away.

Day dawns, filling the beach with the glorious
sights of life,
Sunset hours, twinkling stars, and the beach
shuts its eyes.

The beach sinks in slumber, resting in the arms
of the night.
To be awakened into another tomorrow by the
seagulls' flight.

Beach and ocean, endless love, forever on each
other's side,
Sparkling sand and oceans blue, in togetherness
they abide.

Sail Away

At the darkest hour before the dawn, I stood by
the sea,
The waves were covered in a burnt-grey sky's
canopy.
In the darkness of that hour, there emerged a
lone boat,
With fishermen swaying in motion, to keep the
vessel afloat.
The winter wind made me shiver, but I waited in
a trance,
Watching the men ready their boat, for the ocean
dance.

Fearful of the swelling waves, fearful of that
sombre hour,
I wanted them to wait a while, till the day's
crimson shower.
I called out to them, or so I thought, in my
fearful lost state,
They did not wait or stop for me, for I was not a
sailor's mate.
My whisper didn't reach their ears, my voice did
not carry far,
I stood alone with the sky and sea and a lonely
northern star.

They were not my own brothers, from near or
far-away life,
Yet I felt a oneness with them, I was akin to their
strive.
In a heavy rhythmic motion they pulled their
seasoned oars,
Pulling their tiny vessel far, far away from the
sandy shores.
Their life, fate and friendship entwined with the
waters-deep,
In these waves they learn to dance, to smile and
to weep.

I stood by the shore, watching them sail away
from my vision,
In to the deep, where sky met the sea, or was it
but an illusion.
My heart kept echoing to the dark mist, to raise
its heavy veil,
Pleading with the sun to rise soon, and then
safely they could sail.

Their needs mere and frugal, their hearts filled
with pride,
For each new day they greeted the waves, to
play and to ride.
Like a lover's call the mighty waves thrash on a
barren beach,

To woe a sailor and take him away, far from the
land's reach.
They unite, hidden from our eyes, there where
no one can see,
With no ties of the land, in the lover's arms a
sailor is set free.
In grey fathomless waters, they find rainbow
colours' hue,
The sparkling sun, dressing the sea, in
diamond-studded blue.

They sang in chorus, singing a song of faith and
fortitude,
They oared in symphony, filling hearts, with
sublime gratitude.
I stood quiet, hearing their song, and seeing
them fade away,
The sea was roaring, it was a call, every sailor
must obey.
I stood numbed, seeing them go, bidding a silent
adieu,
They lived a life of glorious challenges, gifted
only to a few.

Run...

Run, run away from home,

Go to Spain, Go to Rome!

On the beaches find your lair,

Live a life full of flair,

Just run away from home.

Where the shackles of constant bickering stare,

Where the ticking clock dares your glare,

Where the pillows carry your sweaty smell,

Where walls with peeling plasters dwell,

Under that dark roof nothing is left of home!

Run, run away from home,

Go to Spain, Go to Rome!

Aging folks all around,

Threatening to curb your thoughts profound.

Like the old owl who has forgotten to fly,

They sit and smirk at whatever you try.

Their fading body, wrinkled mind,

Has long forgotten to be kind.

In such a place you once called home,

Nothing remains of the glorious dome.

So pick up your youth, pick up your jest,

The world beyond is having a fest.

Step out into that amazing world,

Don't wait to see your plans stalled.

Challenges you will face anew,

To hold your hand, just a few.

Yet, march ahead, don't look back,

No matter how heavy gets your sack.

Run, run away from home,

Go to Spain, Go to Rome!

Which House Was It

Which house was it where my first steps seemed
like a mile!
Which house was it where my parents spread
their loving smile!

The roof above my head will change its colour
once more,
With the break of dawn, I will shut another door.
From the walls I have erased all our noisy talk,
From the wilting garden I have plucked each
stalk.

Which house was it where I planted my first sap!
Which house was it where I rocked my baby on
my lap!

'Carpe diem' my love, you had said one day,
Wish you were here to show me the way.
I will lay my shirts in another room tomorrow,
I will line my plates in another kitchen burrow.

Which house was it where I cooked my first
meal!
Which house was it where eating together was a
big deal!

How many houses have I made my home,
How many times have I moved my dome.
The thrashing waves never count the grains of
the sand,
The wandering gypsy never leave their traces on
the land.

Which house was it where we had our first fight!
Which house was it where I stayed up all night!

A favourite cricket bat is chipped from the top,
A discarded pencil heel from the designer shop.
A wall filled with posters, someone's scaling
chart,
Where do I stop, and where do I start.

Which house was it where you first came home
late!
Which house was it where I always waited by
the gate!

I have packed the boxes with memories old and
new,
Many pieces discarded, yet tenderly held back a
few.
The family picture of our first holiday in snow,
Our radiant smiles by the bonfire glow.

Which house was it where I taught the children
to soar high and fly!
Which house was it where I saw them spreading
their wings in the sky!

I will walk another stretch to match your stride,
I will run all the way to be by your side.
A house called home perhaps awaits us by the
lane,
A home we will build with all our love and all
our pain.

Which house is it where we will rest our tired
feet!
Which house is it where all of us will someday
meet!

House

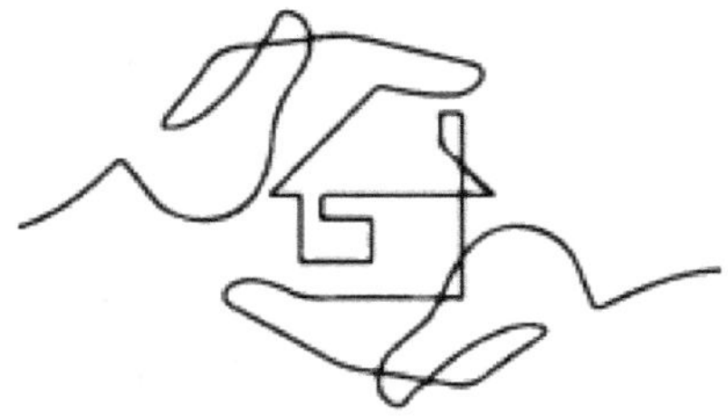

The house looked abandoned and in waiting,
My memories of the house but a few and slowly
fading,
Time had washed away the paint, broken bricks
now lay bared,
But the walls of the house remembered the tales
we had shared,
It was holding on to the memories, I could recall
no more,
Waiting to wake me up with a touch, as I opened
each door.

My childhood like a distant dream was knocking
on my mind,
A hidden treasure grove from a lost world I was
about to find.
Aromas from my Grandma's kitchen softly
drifting in the air,
Forbidden pickle jars atop a shelf, a sweet and
sour affair.

Grandfather on his rocking chair, forever
wearing a frown,
Big wooden stairs creaked as naughty feet ran
up and down.
A tall and jaded corner mirror, always made me
look so small,
An old, rusty cuckoo clock chiming on the front
room wall.
Framed photos of sombre faces, all in black and
white,
An unknown fear gripped the nights, dimmed by
lantern light.
Afternoons in the mango grove, games of hide
and seek,
The cool evening summer breeze, caressing our
hot cheeks.
Years faded the memories, but could not have
torn us apart,
My childhood like a distant dream, half awake in
my heart.

The house had always known, I would find back
my way,
And wake up the sleeping walls with
rainbow-coloured array.
Laughter, cries, warm evenings filling up the
empty rooms,
Playful children, bright flowers making the
garden bloom.

The old and abandoned house, I would bring it
back to life,
The joys known to my childhood, I would once
again revive.

What Will the World Say

The father sat with a hand on his head,
His daughter was sixteen and still unwed.
'What will the world say', was his biggest worry,
He weeped and told the world that he was sorry.

The world kept talking, but time marched on,
The story of the father and daughter soon
forgone.

The young widow wanted to marry her lover,
Her angry parents disowned their own girl,
forever.
'What will the world say', was their big concern,
They could live in grief but not with social
scorn.

The world stopped talking one fine day,
But the daughter had left home to find her way.

His desire to love a man brought him shame,
He was a man of repute, wealth and fame.

'What will the world say', if they got to know,
He hid his real face behind glamor and show.

The world changed again, 'love' finally got its
rights,
Yet, his life was wasted by then, living in secret
frights.

Unhappy in marriage they went on for years,
Divorce was a stigma, they suffered silent tears.
'What will the world say', so they shut their
doors,
They lived in suffering till both their hearts tore.

The world soon laughed, broken marriages were
a norm,
The couple lost their chance, in fear of an
unknown storm.

They believed in different Gods, love was like a
conquest,
Without changing faith their holy union couldn't
be blessed.

'What will the world say', was the only noise
they could hear,
They embraced death, ending love for the Gods
they feared.

The world went on killing and loving in the
name of God,
Faith and religion are still fighting with an
unholy sword.She had her love child out of
wedlock,
Her friends stood by her like a solid rock.
'What will the world say', still came into her life,
To raise her little girl she had to struggle and
strife.

The world saw the rise of a new sun again,
A child is a blessing and cannot be a girl's stain.

'What will the world say', has killed many a
heart,
The world does not matter, it's our story from the
start.
The world will not help us when we need them
most,
The world is like the fear we have of an unseen
ghost.

The world is but people so much like you and
me,
The world is evolving and setting new thoughts
free.

The world will embrace what we teach it to love,
The world will give back to us what we deserve.
Wipe away the tears, guilts, abuse from the
depths of sorrow,
Hold the world's hand and lead it into a new and
better tomorrow.

On the Verge

The cacophony of relentless hammering
thoughts,
Kept echoing in her delirious, confused mind.
A deluge of words, but all twisted in tight knots,
Struggling to hold on, yet breaking in a slow
grind.

She wanted to frame those words in beautiful
lines,
But they kept escaping her, it felt just like
treason.
She wanted to evoke her faithful words sublime,
But her words were gone without any reason.

She sensed she was forgetting to remember,
Her days were no more clearer than her nights.
With each day she felt like a dying ember,
Fleeting memories vanishing in bright light.

The people had flocked from far and wide,
They were eager to hear her speak.
They had waited long by her ailing side,
But she could feel, her chances were bleak.

Her eyes once twinkled with abundance of life,
Those empty eyes now searched their face.
Trying to remember her own story of strife,
To reach out once more for some lost trace.

In this vast emptiness one thought kept
knocking,
Remembering a voice, a promise, amidst this
dilution.
Perhaps he was a lie, her memories merely
mocking,
Like her tales, he was but a figment of her
imagination.

She kept staring blankly, his face drifting near
and far,
From this pain of oblivion, no one could give
her relief.
Now so lost, but once she was a poetess, a rising
star,
And in her eyes now reflected deep empty pools
of grief.

Waiting people; their impatience, their
restlessness,
She could feel it spreading through her room.
Their failed disguise, their hidden distress,
Hushed whispers of the impending gloom.

Through all the pain of incoherent loss, she
waited,
She waited for him to reach her door, one day.
Through all her struggle of remembering forever
muted,
She would not know, it was her words that had
pushed him away.

Solitude

Solitude, you are the lone bird above, soaring
high,
You are the caged bird, desiring to reach the sky,
You are the first drop of rain, on a parched piece
of land,
You are imprisoned, in an hourglass, like a grain
of sand.

Solitude, you are in my mother's eyes, waiting
tirelessly for me,
You are in someone's broken heart, weeping
alone, by the sea,
You are in a little boy's smile, when he sees the
shooting star,
You are in the old man's stride, walking
homeward, very far.

Solitude, you are in the midnight silence, of a
busy city street,
You are in those countless waves, thrashing at
the rock's feet,
You are in that crimson light of dawn, waking up
from sleep,
You are hiding like a tiny teardrop, lost in the
ocean's deep.

Solitude, you are with a lone soldier, on guard,
near the fence,
You are in a sailor's heart, searching the shore
with his lens,
You are on a poet's mind, amongst the hills and
meadows,
You are a silent prayer by the night, with a
grieving widow.

Solitude, you are in the echoing chants of
Gurbani, by the day,
You are in the evening azan, welcoming the
evening to stay,
You are in the shlokas, flowing like music in a
melodious voice,
You are sitting within the Chappell, tuning to my
inward noise.

Solitude, you are in my absolute silence, you are
in my chaos,
You are in my joyful reverie, you are laced with
pathos,
You are in my drama, you are in my shameless
fall and peak,
Solitude, you are my treasured companion, it is
you I forever seek.

Lost Words

My words are knocking at my door,
And I am not ready to hear.
My words are waiting on a cold floor,
And I am numbed with fear.
My words await like a lover forlorn,
Aah, for the love of my words, I am torn.

I remember closing the door on your face,
Not with a loud thud, but with gentle grace.
Like one hides after losing the race,
I wanted to hide in an agonizing space.
You once attempted to hold me back,
But I had vanished in my ink-blue black.

Why should I bring you inside?
What is there for you to see?

The same stories of broken pride,
Chasing the ego and no place to hide.
The opium-laced hours of mundane,
Crossing the borders of sane-insane.
A few broken images of the bygone day,
Effortlessly piling upon my today.
With no ray of light lighting up tomorrow,
Yesterday's happiness drowning in sorrow.

Why should I bring you inside?
What is there for you to see?

Smiles and laughter I once had spread,
Those books together, we once had read.
The pages are torn, flying around the room,
The air is dismal, laden with gloom.
Unopened pages are crying in vain,
They look at me, but with disdain.
Memories are fading, without any fanfare,
And I sit in silence, within these walls of
despair.

Why should I bring you inside?
What is there for you to see?

There is no novella to tell or bard to mourn,
There is a numbing silence, to which I have
sworn.
The stories we had once weaved together,
The dreams made of wings as light as feather,
They have flown away from my mind,
Not to come back, and no one to remind.
All grand and lofty words sublime,
Have been buried in the ruins of time.

Why do you still stand at my door,
My long-forgotten words candor.
Words with power, to build and destroy,
To lure and win is your age-old ploy.
You unfurl stories from my heart,
You hold me tight and tear me apart.
My thoughts had frozen like winter snow,
Your sunshine awakens with a tender glow.

My words are knocking at my door,
Alas, I will make you wait no more.
Like a diver from the depths of sea,
Bringing the pearl and setting it free,
My words you pull me from my reverie,
Like a shameless lover's ecstasy.

Colourless

Have you seen the northern lights,
Dancing hues in sheer delight,
Some creator, with a torch in hand,
Making them dance, like a celestial band.
On the skies canvas, soaked with rain,
The creator, splashes some colours in vain,
Vibgyor is tied with an invisible string,
As a sun-kissed rainbow spreads its wings.
The sun sets and scarlet colours rush,
To hide the sun, in an orange blush,
The creator smiles, with a brush in hand,
He wants to paint the skies and land.
The crystal blue skies or the sombre greys,
The creator's moods, he clearly displays,
Even through the darkest of the nights,
There is a twinkling star giving us light.
Our creator, so benevolent and great,
Why do you turn blind to the blind's fate?
Depriving them the world's magical sights,
Why are their days forever cursed as nights?

Till I fall

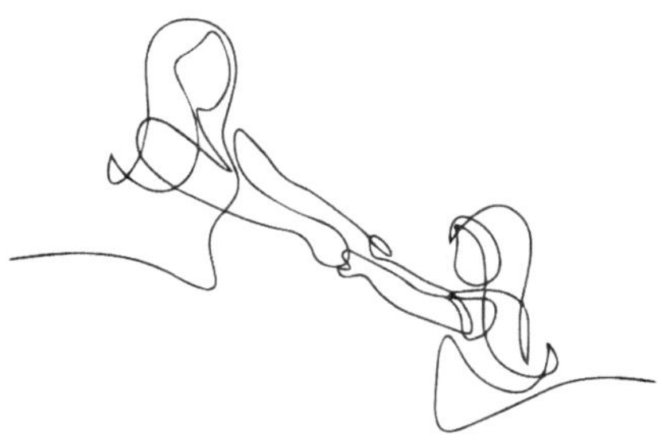

The dust of time has settled on my leaf,
The dust of years heavily laden with grief.
No monsoon rain can wash me clean,
No summer sun can give me back my sheen.
I stood the tests of earth, holding to my roots,
I saved all the zest of spring for my offshoots.
Till you learn to reach the root I will hold your
branch,
Till you learn to spread the green, my leaf will
not blanch.
In your shining reflection I see the hope of
tomorrow,
In your swaying motion I see vanishing waves
of sorrow.
When my last leaf will touch the ground without
any noise,
Remember, here once stood a tree, with deep
strength and poise.

Unmatched

You ask for my story, my sweet love,
Aah, where do I begin, where do I stop!

Did my story begin on the day of my birth?
Was it a joyful occasion, filled with mirth?
Or was I the abandoned child of my father,
Cause of pain, shame or pride to my mother.
I cannot give you a lineage sparkling clean,
But I can promise, a future with joyous sheen.

You ask for my story, my sweet love,
Aah, where do I begin, where do I stop!

I was this charismatic lover, all my life,
For women and money I never did strife.
Was I a social stigma, or a gallant knight?
Did people throng around me with respect or
fright?
You look at me askance with your innocent eyes,
But my answers can only whisper silent cries.

You ask for my story, my sweet love,
Aah, where do I begin, where do I stop!

You walked into my life, a beautiful, fragile
dream,
Drenching me softly, in an overflowing stream.
I can chant your name with ecstasy all night,
And wake up to your gentle face, cradled by
sunlight.
For a lady of your stature, I may not be worthy,
Will you still keep me forever, I humbly implore
thee.

You ask for my story, my sweet love,
Aah, where do I begin, where do I stop!

When they will call you my darling, by my
name,
Will it bring you honour or will you shy with
shame?
I do not have the power to add to your glory,
My poorly designed life is a series of misery.
Yet I seek your love, it is indeed my selfish
desire,
To dance and burn by your side, I'm a beetle
around fire.

You ask for my story, my sweet love,
Aah, where do I begin, where do I stop!

Like a beggar waiting for alms, I wait at your
door,
With your one tender look, my life feels
restored.
You ask me one simple question, in return of
your love,
My life's fragmented story, only the heaven
knows above.
Together we could weave our dreamland of
passion,
Yet, you seek to dive deep, into my past
commotion.

You ask for my story, my sweet love,
Aah, where do I begin, where do I stop!

Come to me my dearest, hold your questions
afar,
I will wait for you till eternity, my doors open
ajar.
Horses and carriages, old mansions by the lake,
The pleasures of the riches will be for yours to
take.
The rubies on your neck, your bangles opaque
jade,
With time my darling their dazzle shall fade.

You ask for my story, my sweet love,
Aah, where do I begin, where do I stop!

My devotion to your love will stand the test of
time,
Way beyond the glorious days of our youthful
prime.
I make no promises to live forever in a blissful
home,
But holding hands, the world around, we will
roam.
Our path will glitter with the stars and the
morning lights,
We will seal our story with a gentle kiss on
wakeful nights.

You ask for my story, my sweet love,
Aah, this is where I begin,
And this is where I stop.

Album

The time keeper of yesteryears, photos resting in an album,
Lost but not completely forgotten in life's busy humdrum.
One such album full of sepia photos, on the table it laid,
To open it and trying to remember, she was a little afraid.
The fragile pages of the album, were almost crumbling,
Her memories of those past days, were slowly stumbling.
Pictures of friends, families, moments, forever locked,
On the verge of remembering it all, her memories mocked.
She tried hard to remember, each photo one by one,
But her failing mind kept forgetting the days that were done.
The pictures were old and fraying, with stories of past time,
Yet she knew this was once her beautiful world sublime.

This thought itself was enough, to bring tears to
her eyes,
With a soft smile she closed the album, for it
was time to bid goodbye.

9 789360 940997